Kane Simons is a barrister at 18 St John Chambers in Manchester specialising in personal injury litigation. He has a particular interest in claims involving cyclists, motorcyclists and pedestrians.

# A Practical Guide to The Law and Regulation of E-Bikes and E-Scooters

# A Practical Guide to The Law and Regulation of E-Bikes and E-Scooters

Kane Simons, Barrister

Law Brief Publishing

Published 2022 by Law Brief Publishing, an imprint of Law Brief Publishing Ltd
30 The Parks
Minehead
Somerset
TA24 8BT

www.lawbriefpublishing.com

Paperback: 978-1-914608-35-3

# PREFACE

For simplicity, throughout this book I have used the common term 'e-bike' as a catch-all term for electrically assisted pedal cycles and the term 'e-scooter' to define electric stand-up scooters.

The case law and legislation referred to in this book are correct as of 1st July 2022, however as part of their legislative agenda for 2022 and 2023, the Government have stated their intention to legalise and regulate the use of e-scooters by way of a forthcoming Transport Bill. The details of such a bill have yet to be announced. Assuming it becomes law, it will have a significant effect upon how e-scooter users are treated in both the civil and criminal courts in England and Wales.

To that end, many of the laws and regulations as set out in this book will soon be out of date. It is intended that a second edition will be published soon. If any readers have suggestions, practical advice or are aware of any helpful cases that readers may wish to know, please feel free to contact me.

Kane Simons
July 2022

# CONTENTS

# Introduction

The law and regulation of e-bikes and e-scooters is messy and often incoherent. The discourse is plagued with misinformation from retailers and the media as well as inconsistent approaches to enforcement. It is further complicated by a constantly shifting regulatory framework that struggles to keep up with advances in consumer technology.

The book aims to set out the law and regulation of e-scooters and e-bikes in a simple and straightforward manner, with a focus on accidents and insurance.

# PART ONE

# E-SCOOTERS

## Micromobility Devices

Improvements in battery and motor technology have led to a proliferation of new forms of personal transport that do not sit easily within any of the traditional categories for motor vehicles. Examples include 'hoverboards', Segways, electric skateboards and electric unicycles. In official parlance, these tend to be known as 'micromobility devices' or 'personal light electric vehicles'. The most popular type these devices is the upright, electric scooter, commonly known as the e-scooter.

Micromobility devices offer a range of advantages to the consumer: they are small, light and cheap to run, and as an alternative to cars and motorcycles they are a means of travel with a very low carbon footprint. Further, like bicycles or e-bikes they have the potential to reduce traffic and congestion.

Until very recently, no specific laws governed the use of micromobility devices and their use has continued unregulated. A lack of legislation has led to confusion for consumers, motorists, police forces and the courts.

# A Motor Vehicle?

In the absence of any clear statute specifically dealing with micromobility devices, the primary source of legislation is the Road Traffic Act 1988 which sets out, amongst other things, obligations for road users, in particular the users of motor vehicles.

For example, under s87(1) of the Road Traffic Act 1988, it is an offence to drive on a road a motor vehicle of any class otherwise in accordance with a licence. Similarly, under s143(1), a driver of a motor vehicle is obliged to have third-party insurance when driving on a road.

A motor vehicle is defined in section 185(1)(c) as *'a mechanically propelled vehicle intended or adapted for use on roads'*. Exceptions and subcategories are carved out for mobility scooters, tractors, motorcycles and other varieties of established motor vehicles. However, in the context of new types of vehicle, this definition has had to be interpreted by courts.

On the face of it, micromobility devices are mechanically propelled. The real issue is whether they are *'intended or adapted for use on roads'*.

## Burns v Currell

We may think of e-scooters and micromobility devices as very modern inventions. However, some of the relevant case law goes back as far as 60 years ago. The case of Burns v Currell [1963] 2 QB 433 concerns David Burns, who in September 1962 was caught driving a Go-Kart on a quiet industrial road in High Wycombe. He was charged and convicted of a series of regulatory offences and fined £5, 4s. He appealed to the High Court by way of case stated.

The main issue for the Court to consider was whether the Go-Kart *was 'intended or adapted for use on roads for the purposes of section 253 of the Road Traffic Act 1960'* (since replaced by section 185 of the Road Traffic Act 1988).

It was held that the test to be applied was whether a reasonable person looking at the vehicle would say that one of its users would be a road user, or whether some general use on the roads was contemplated by a user.

In the context of the Go-Kart, the justices found that there was no evidence that people tended to use these on the road and there was no such material before the Court at first instance that would have allowed the bench to be sure as to be able to convict. The result was in the context of this particular case, the Go-Kart was not considered to be a vehicle intended or adapted for use on roads.

## Chief Constable of Avon and Somerset Constabulary v F

This case ([1987] 1 All E.R. 318) concerned the use of a 'scrambler' motorcycle. The motorcycle had been originally built for road use but had since been adapted for off-road use by removing the registration plates, lights and speedometer. It was not insured.

The defendant had been caught by the police pushing this bike on a public road and was charged with several contraventions of the Road Traffic Act 1972. He was acquitted and the prosecutor appealed by way of case stated. As part of the grounds of appeal, it was suggested that the motorcycle – despite its modifications – was still a motor vehicle for the purposes of the Act.

The Court emphasised that the test in Burns v Currell was based upon the view of the 'reasonable person', not the particular user of the vehicle. Nevertheless, the Court at first instance had enough information to find on the facts that the vehicle had been adapted such that a reasonable person would not anticipate some road use. Accordingly, it was not a motor vehicle intended or adapted for use on roads.

## Percy v Smith

This case ([1986] RTR 252) concerned a forklift truck. The truck had been insured for use on the road and occasionally used on the roads to travel between industrial sites by a previous owner.

The driver of the truck was stopped and the driver was charged with regulatory crimes relating to a worn tyre tread. The defendant contended that the truck was not intended or adapted for use on public roads and was therefore not a motor vehicle. He was convicted and appealed to the Divisional Court.

On appeal, the justices dismissed the appeal. They had applied the test in Burns v Currell and concluded that it was a motor vehicle for the purposes of the Act.

This case marks a turning point in the case law where the test as set out in Burns starts to be applied very broadly. As long as a reasonable person might anticipate some use on the road, a vehicle could be considered a motor vehicle for the purposes of the Act.

# Chief Constable of the North Yorkshire Police v Michael Saddington

One of the earliest cases involving a modern form of personal transport was Saddington [2000] EWHC Admin 409. In 1999 Mr Saddington was charged with regulatory offences after being caught riding an unregistered and uninsured scooter on the road in Harrogate without a licence. The scooter he was riding was called a 'Go-Ped', an early incarnation of the modern electric standing scooter, albeit one powered by a small two-stroke engine mounted on the footboard. It was capable of travelling up to 20mph on a flat surface.

The issue for the Divisional Court was whether the Go-Ped was a motor vehicle '*intended or adapted for use on the road*' for the purposes of section 185 of the 1988 Act. If it was such a motor vehicle, it would require insurance and registration, just like a traditional motorcycle.

The Go-Ped was hardly a traditional road vehicle; it had no lights, no suspension and no indicators. It was also marketed as an executive toy rather than a means of road transport. Further, it was not practical as an off-road vehicle as it required a flat surface in order to move at a useful speed. Mr Saddington accepted that it was not compliant with the the applicable construction and use regulations and argued the point that as a toy, it was clearly not meant for use on the road.

Adopting the test in Burns v Currell, the opinion of the justices at first instance was that a reasonable person *would* consider Mr Saddington to have been a road user.

The Divisional Court agreed and found on the facts that it was a vehicle likely to be used on the road (indeed, Mr Saddington was using it on the road) and therefore the rider's conviction stood. It did not matter that the scooter was particularly unroadworthy or did not comply with the relevant construction and use regulations for motorcycles. Nor did it matter that a road was not necessarily the main place the vehicle might be used.

There is some discussion in the judgment as to the long-term implications of this decision. Pill LJ asked counsel what would happen if someone wished to register, plate and insure a Go-Ped. The issue was not considered in detail and it was decided these were matters for the Ministry of Transport rather than the courts.

## Director of Public Prosecutions v Paul Matthew King

Perhaps the first case involving a truly modern micromobility device was that of King v DPP [2008] EWHC Admin 447. Mr King was charged with driving a 'City Mantis' on the road without insurance. Although the judgment gives little detail about the nature of the City Mantis, it appears to have been an early personal electric transport – a battery-powered folding mini-motorcycle that was cutting-edge technology in 2008.

Reading the judgment, it seems that the police, the CPS and the Court were unfamiliar with this type of product and felt obliged to follow the statute and existing case law, which defined it as a motor vehicle for use on roads.

By this point, the case law suggests that nearly any new form of micromobility device would meet the Burns test.

## Coates v CPS

One of the most famous early micromobility device was the Segway, a stand-up scooter first sold in 2001 that was able to steer and remain upright through the use of internal gyroscopes. Segways did not look like any transport that had come before and classification was far from clear. As it was not obviously a road vehicle, a Mr Coates decided to ride his on the pavement in Barnsley. In the case of Coates [2011] EWHC Admin 2032 he was charged under section 72 of the Highways Act 1835 for driving a carriage on the footway. He appealed his conviction but lost. Again, the High Court found that the vehicle was intended for use on the road and therefore could not be ridden on the pavement.

## Conclusions

The case law shows that micromobility devices fall between two stools. They cannot be ridden on the road as they require insurance and registration. However, because they have a motor they cannot be ridden on the pavement either. As insurance or plating of micromobility devices and electric scooters is not viable (each make and model would have to be 'type approved' as a motorcycle by the Driver and Vehicle Standards Agency (DVSA) before use on the road, and even then it might be difficult to find an insurer willing to provide insurance) the result is that nearly all such devices cannot be used legally anywhere other than on private land.

# Purchasing E-Scooters

Despite the above restrictions on the use of e-scooters and other micromobility devices, there is very little to stop retailers and importers from selling them in Britain. As they remain technically legal to ride on private land, there are no restrictions on who can purchase or sell them. The result is that one can very easily purchase e-scooters from high street and online retailers.

In the absence of regulation, there are no established standards. For example, some imported e-scooters can travel at very high speeds. There are no requirements for bells, brakes, lights and no specific requirements for build quality or construction.

Most mainstream retailers will import e-scooters from other jurisdictions with established construction regulations. Mainstream retailers tend to sell e-scooters restricted to 15.5mph and 350 watts of power. However, there is nothing to stop specialist retailers producing or importing high-powered e-scooters with a power output of up to 8000 watts, with most having around 350 watts. In the absence of an established regulatory framework, these scooters are treated by law the same as those with a more modest power output.

It is notable that most retailers selling e-scooters and micromobility devices feel obliged to tell consumers of their legal status. For example, when purchasing an e-scooter online from high-street retailer Halfords, there is a very visible warning at the top of the webpage stating that the vehicle is *'not to be used on public roads, cycle paths or pavements'*. There is then a link to a further page setting out a broad summary of the law[1].

---

[1] https://www.halfords.com/cycling/advice/are-electric-scooters-legal.html

The result is confusion for consumers who are at once invited to purchase such devices whilst being told that they are not allowed to use them.

# Rental E-Scooters

## An Introduction

There were three main factors that led to the introduction in 2020 of rental e-scooters that could be legally used on British streets.

The first was the success of rental schemes in other jurisdictions; a viable business model existed and there were companies interested in expanding their services into the British market. Companies such as Lime (also known as Neutron Holdings Inc.) and Bird had established schemes in the 2010s in cities across the world whereby individuals could rent e-scooters. Rental schemes generally followed a standard model whereby dock-less electric scooters would be left around a city. Users would install an application on their smartphone which indicated a map of nearby scooters and would allow them to unlock and use them for a fee. Using GPS, the rental companies could charge customers per mile or per minute. By 2019, large-scale schemes were present in cities as diverse as Singapore, New York and Paris.

The second was a creeping realisation by the Government that there was little that could be done to stop the use of e-scooters on the road and that it would make sense to legalise and regulate their use.

The third was the Covid-19 pandemic, which led to a significant reduction in public transport capacity due to the need for social distancing. Planned trials for the regulation of e-scooters were expedited. It was hoped that rental e-scooters would help ease the burden on public transport systems in a way that benefitted public health. In March 2020, the Government published the Future of Transport Regulatory Review which looked at the opportunity and risks of legalising micromobility devices. The pandemic caused plans to explore the legalisation of e-scooters to be rushed into effect.

Rather than sweeping legalisation, a cautious approach was taken; the plan was to introduce a pilot scheme limited to rental e-scooters only. Trials would then be implemented from which evidence could be gathered that could inform future policy.

## Electric Scooter Trials and Traffic Signs (Coronavirus) Regulations and General Directions 2020

The Electric Scooter Trials and Traffic Signs (Coronavirus) Regulations and General Directions 2020 ("the Regulations") were hastily introduced in June 2020 after a short consultation period and came into force on the $4^{th}$ of July of the same year.

The effect of the Regulations was to create a new class of vehicle, subject to its own regulation. The government's aim was to regulate e-scooters in as similar way as possible to e-bikes whereby a new discrete class of vehicle is created by statute. However, unlike electric pedal cycles, the use of e-scooters is limited to those hired out as part of a rental scheme.

Such rentals are limited to a trial scheme in which an arrangement is made between one or more public authorities and a '*person who hires out electric scooters*'. A company cannot legally rent out e-scooters except through a local authority procurement exercise (and with permission from the Department for Transport).

The prevalence of a particular type of stand-up, electric scooter internationally appears to have informed the Regulations. Of all the micromobility devices that the government could have adopted for the scheme, they have simply chosen the most common and most popular.

## *Regulation 2*

Regulation 2 amends the Road Vehicles (Registration and Licencing) Regulations 2002 to eliminate the need for registration of an e-scooter, so long as it is being used as part of a trial arranged with a Local Authority. Regulation 2(3)(b) provides a set of requirements for a compliant e-scooter. It follows that if an e-scooter does not comply with the requirements, it is not considered an electric scooter for the purposes of the law and is simply considered a generic motor vehicle. The obligations are as follows:

### *Requirement (a): Power*

The scooter is to be fitted with an electric motor with a maximum continuous power rating not exceeding 500 watts. Note that this is *double* the power rating of a legal pedal assisted cycle, despite e-scooters travelling around the same speed. In the context of a rental scooter that will be used all day without the need for charging it is anticipated that very large batteries will be required, adding weight to the scooter. The extra power is simply required to move the vehicle.

### *Requirement (b): No pedals*

The electric scooters cannot have pedals capable of propelling the vehicle. To allow this would create a grey area between electric scooters and electric bikes.

### *Requirement (c): Wheel alignment*

The scooters also have to have two wheels – one front and one rear, aligned along the direction of travel. This is the standard form for e-scooters elsewhere and allows the rental companies to import scooters from other jurisdictions. It also prevents the usage of other types of micromobility device such as unicycles and 'hoverboards', which might be less stable or more difficult to ride.

### *Requirement (d): Capacity*

The scooters must be designed to carry no more than one person

### *Requirement (e): Weight*

The maximum weight (not including the driver) must not exceed 55kg. Note that modern e-bikes are no longer subject to a weight requirement; this probably reflects the need for larger e-bikes such as cargo bikes, something that is not required in the context of e-scooters.

### *Requirement (f): Speed*

The maximum design speed must not exceed 15.5mph. This is similar to the maximum powered speed for legal e-bikes. However, e-bikes can potentially travel faster than this under pedal power. As part of the consultation prior to the drafting of the Regulations, it was anticipated that the speed of the scooters would be limited to 12.5mph, however the government increased the figure in response to a preference for a higher speed.

### *Requirement (g): Control of direction*

The scooters must have a means of directional control through the use of handlebars mechanically linked to the steered wheel. Again, this is a prescribed form and shape that restricts the use of hoverboards, skateboards and Segways.

### *Requirement (h): Control of speed*

The scooters must have a means of controlling the speed through hand controls, in other words a throttle. This again rules out the use of some other micromobility devices such as hoverboards and Segways that control their speed through the movements of the user.

*Requirement (i): Power defaults to off*

The scooters must have a power control that defaults to the off position. In practice, this means that if a rider lets go of the handlebars, the scooter will come to stop. This is meant as a safety mechanism.

## *Regulation 3*

Regulation 3 amends the Motor Cycle (Protective Helmets) Regulations 1998 to remove the need for helmets when riding an electric scooter when used as part of a trial. The government has provided guidance that recommends the use of a helmet but has not made use mandatory – much as with bicycles and e-bikes.

## *Regulation 4*

Regulation 4 amends the Motor Vehicle (Driving Licences) Regulations 1999 to authorise the use of electric scooters when used as part of a trial, provided that the rider has a provisional driving licence. There is no need for basic moped or motorcycle training.

## *Regulation 5*

Regulation 5 amends the Traffic Signs Regulations 2016 to allow electric scooters to be used in cycle lanes when used as part of a trial. It also clarifies that any signs relating to pedal cycles will also represent e-scooters.

## *Other Controls*

Local authorities also can add their own requirements for the trials, for example restricting the number of and location of scooters, providing helmets, training and mandating the sharing of data between the rental company and local authority.

Further, a vehicle special order (VSO) has been published that adds certain technical requirements from rental companies, for example anti-tampering devices, audible warnings, braking systems, lights and minimum stability requirements.

## Effect of the Regulations

The Regulations are not drafted broadly. They set out a very defined and narrow type of scooter that can be used. More importantly, they limit who can use them; the requirement to have a provisional driving licence prevents under 16s from renting them and creates an extra hurdle for tourists.

Notably, the Regulations do not remove the need for mandatory third-party insurance. The author suspects that this is the reason why the trial has taken the form of a rental scheme; the insurance costs can be baked into the price of the rental in a way that they cannot with private scooters. It also eliminated the need to create a whole new market for e-scooter insurance at the height of the pandemic.

The Explanatory Memorandum to the Regulations suggests that participating local authorities will run trials of 12 months each and allow data to be gathered from the rental operators. The trial scheme has since been extended to November 2022.

In the 2022 Queen's Speech, the Government announced as part of a forthcoming Transport Bill that privately owned e-scooters will be legalised for road use, although the details have yet to be revealed. The implication is that the Trial has been deemed a success by those in power and that there is a willingness to expand the use of e-scooters more generally.

# Criminal Law

## Penalties

In practice, the criminal penalties for riding a privately-owned e-scooter or micromobility device on the public highway are likely to take the form of a Fixed Penalty Notice.

The offence of driving without insurance carries a fixed penalty of £300 and six penalty points on a driving licence. If the matter proceeds to Court, the offence is summary only. Depending on the seriousness of the offence, the magistrates' court has the power to impose an unlimited fine, up to eight penalty points or disqualification from driving for up to a year. Aggravating features relevant to sentencing will include:

- where use has led to an accident or damage;
- never having passed a driving test;
- giving false details;
- using the scooter for work; and
- evidence of sustained use.

The offence of driving without an appropriate licence carries a fixed penalty of £100 and three to six penalty points.

It is also worth noting that riders of e-scooters are also able to be prosecuted for other motoring offences such riding on a pavement, failing to comply with traffic signals, using a mobile phone and drink driving.

Speeding offences are relatively unlikely as most e-scooters for sale in the UK are limited to 15.5mph in a similar manner to e-bikes as they have been imported from other jurisdictions with similar speed restrictions. Even the fastest e-scooters are unlikely to be able to travel more than 40mph.

## Seizures

Section 165A of the Road Traffic Act 1988 gives the police powers to seize vehicles that are driven without a licence and/or insurance. In the context of a privately-owned e-scooter being ridden on the public highway, it is extremely unlikely, if not impossible that the rider is insured. There will be a clear legal path to seizure in nearly all cases.

Section 59 of the Police Reform Act 2002 also allows for the seizure of vehicles that are being used in a manner that is causing or is likely to cause alarm, distress or annoyance.

The use of seizures appears to have been a common tactic by police forces, with some advertising a high volume of seizures.

## Local bans

Whilst the use of e-scooters can be legal on private land with the landowner's permission, it is also open for local landowners to restrict the use of e-scooters.

Recent examples include Transport for London, which in December 2021 banned the use of e-scooters and e-unicycles on its services and premises, ostensibly due to the fire risk caused by lithium-ion batteries.

## Enforcement

As well as mixed messages when it comes to purchasing e-scooters, there are further inconsistencies of approach when it comes to enforcement.

The case law as set out above should have marked the death-knell for private micromobility device use in England and Wales. If a person could neither ride on the road nor the pavement, such devices are not viable as a useful form of transport. The reality though, is that the benefits they confer to consumers render these devices too practical and attractive not to be used.

The result is a barrage of mixed messages from retailers, the Government, the media and police forces.

Although the case law points in one direction, the last few years have seen a decline in the enforcement of such laws. A good example is of the approach taken by the Metropolitan Police in London. At the date of publication, the Metropolitan Police's policy appears to be that they will only seize e-scooters if they are being ridden in an antisocial manner. The inference seems to be that because there are so many e-scooters being used, the seizing of such devices would be a disproportionate use of police time and resources.

With forthcoming legalisation and regulation, it is even less likely that police forces will continue to charge e-scooter users for simple regulatory offences to any great degree.

# Claims by E-Scooter Riders

## Floodgates opening?

With the number of e-scooter riders increasing, it is foreseeable that the number of claims involving injured riders will likewise increase. While no statistics are available, anecdotally, personal injury solicitors appear to be seeing such claims more frequently.

Riders of e-scooters are vulnerable to injury due to fast acceleration, small wheels and a high centre of gravity.

Whilst the basic issues of negligence and breach of duty remain the same as with other road users, the novelty and potential illegality of e-scooters has led to insurers adopting novel arguments in response to claims brought by riders.

## *Ex turpi causa*

With nearly all e-scooters (and many e-bikes) being ridden illegally, it is foreseeable that when a claimant is injured whilst riding one (for example, being hit by a car or striking a pothole and falling) a defendant might raise an *ex turpi causa non oritur actio* defence. The general rule on illegality is that a claimant ought not to benefit from pursuing a criminal enterprise. In that context, it is easy to foresee an insurer or the Motor Insurers' Bureau ('MIB') refusing to compensate on the grounds that a rider is committing a criminal act.

If a claim is brought by the rider of an e-scooter (or indeed a non-compliant e-bike), it may be useful for a defendant to explicitly plead the potential crimes committed by the claimant. Any resulting finding or admission could be used not only to assist with *ex turpi causa* arguments, it could also used tactically against the claimant. For example, a defendant could threaten to report such acts to the claimant's motor insurer (if they are a driver) or even to the police[2].

A example list of regulatory criminal acts to plead might include the following:

- Driving a motor vehicle on a road or public place without a policy of insurance, contrary to section 143 of the Road Traffic Act 1988;

- Driving a motor vehicle on a road without a licence authorising him to drive a motor vehicle of that class, contrary to section 87(1) of the Road Traffic Act 1988;

- Driving on a footpath, contrary to section 72 of the Highway Act 1835;

- Riding a mechanically-propelled vehicle in a cycle lane or mixed-use path, contrary to section 34 of the Road Traffic Act 1988; and

- Riding a motorcycle without a protective helmet, contrary to regulation 4(1) of the Motor Cycles (Protective Helmets) Regulations 1998.

Other breaches might include those relating to number-plates, type approval, MOT certificates and vehicle registration. These are unlikely

[2] It should be noted that most of these crimes are summary only offences and therefore any charges have to be laid within six months of the offence. When advising a claimant, it may be sensible to wait until after this period before notifying a defendant of a claim.

to add much to a claim when considered alongside those more serious breaches listed above.

At the date of publication, no cases of this nature have appeared before the higher courts. However, given the high volume of people injured on e-scooters, it is likely to be only a matter of time. By looking at similar cases, we can anticipate the approach likely to be taken by the judiciary.

Fortunately for claimants, in the context of road traffic accidents, the *ex turpi causa* defence is a difficult one to establish. In the Court of Appeal case of McCracken v Smith & Others [2015] EWCA Civ 380 for example, the claimant was riding pillion on an un-plated, unregistered, stolen, off-road motorcycle being driven dangerously in a cycle lane when it was struck by a car. The Court found that the fact that the claimant was travelling in breach of the law had nothing to do with the negligence of the driver who collided with him. The relationship between the claimant's turpitude (his participation in the joint enterprise to ride the bike dangerously) and the negligence of the driver was not such as to debar the claim. However, the causal contribution of the dangerous riding of the bike (for which the claimant was responsible) was to be taken into account in the assessment of his contributory negligence. This approach was adopted again in a later case called Clark v Farley [2018] EWHC 1007.

A helpful way to look at the potential approach of the judiciary is to consider the judgment in Wallett v Vickers [2018] EWHC 3008 (QB). In this case, a claim was brought by the family of a deceased driver who died in a collision after racing with another driver on a public street. The defendant insurer argued that the deceased was guilty of the offence of dangerous driving and therefore any claim by his estate and dependants was based upon that turpitude and ought to be barred. The claimants argued that this was an issue of contributory negligence only.

In considering his judgment Males J (at paragraph 38) had to consider whether all criminal offences prevented the recovery of damages:

> *"...careless driving is a criminal offence but nobody would suggest that careless driving by the claimant prevents the recovery of damages (reduced as appropriate on account of contributory negligence) in a road traffic case where both drivers are partly to blame. In such a case the recovery of damages does not offend public notions of the fair distribution of resources and poses no threat to the integrity of the law. On the contrary, the recovery of damages is in accordance with public policy. The claimant is not compensated for the consequence of his own criminal act. Rather, as a result of the reduction for contributory fault, he is compensated only for that part of the damage which the law regards as having been caused by the defendant's negligence."*

To many personal injury lawyers, this will ring true. There are many cases involving minor car accidents, for example, where both a claimant and defendant driver will have been driving carelessly and one or both will recover damages. Also, no one suggests that a speeding driver is barred from recovering damages, or indeed an injured person who happens to be driving an uninsured vehicle.

There is an argument to be made that the core criminal acts committed by the rider of a privately-owned e-scooter are simply regulatory; the police tend to charge riders with *driving without insurance*. After all, e-scooters can be ridden legally if rented and insured.

This is arguably a far less serious criminal offence than *dangerous driving,* which can carry a custodial sentence. If in the above cases, the more serious offence did not give rise to an *ex turpi causa* defence, it is very unlikely that a court would find that the less serious offences of driving without insurance or otherwise in accordance with a licence would debar riders from recovering damages.

It is possible that if an e-scooter was ridden in a particularly anti-social manner, for example whilst the rider was intoxicated, speeding and/or banned from driving, the severity of the criminal activity would be enough to justify debarring him from recovering damages. Such turpitude would have to be more significant than in McCracken. Further, if a claimant is riding a vastly overpowered or inherently dangerous micromobility device there may be good arguments in favour of the defendant.

A specific case involving e-scooters has yet to come before the higher courts and it may well be that a court would find that different standard of care applies to riders of e-scooters, as opposed to cars or traditional motorcycles. In the absence of legislation, it is largely a matter of public policy as to how the riders of privately-owned e-scooters are approached by the judiciary. It may well be that a court finds that simply by riding one the turpitude of a potential claimant is worse than that of a car driver who, for example, decides to race. In that situation, it is possible that a claim could fail on the grounds of illegality.

## *Ex turpi causa* – individual heads of loss

An increasingly common practice is for defendants not to plead illegality generally as a barrier to succeeding in a claim, but to raise it in relation to specific heads of loss.

A common tactic from defendant insurers is to admit liability generally where a claimant has been injured on an e-scooter (usually after being struck by a car), but to deny recoverability of the repair/replacement costs of the e-scooter on the grounds that any replacement would be used illegally.

This is a public policy decision, and it is unclear how the Courts will approach it.

When it comes to specific heads of loss being challenged for illegality, most of the relevant case law comes in the context of credit hire. In Agheampong v Allied Manufacturing (London) Ltd [2008] 6 WLUK 740 for example, an uninsured driver brought a claim for credit hire after his car was damaged in an accident. The claim failed on the basis that to replace a car which the claimant could not have driven legally would have led to further crimes being committed. It is notable that it was found on the facts that the claimant had deliberately misled the court regarding his intention to insure the car. It is also notable that at no point was the recoverability of repair costs challenged. It is arguable that when it comes to this sort of case Agheampong can be distinguished; there is usually no deliberate attempt to mislead and a claim for replacement/repair is very different from a claim for credit hire.

There are also inconsistent County Court decisions on other issues, such as whether the lack of an MOT will prevent the recoverability of hire claims.

In the context of e-scooters, the issue does not appear to have come before the Courts on appeal or in any reported judgment. If the Courts were to consider the issue, the nature of e-scooters would have to be considered in the context of public policy, applying the test in Patel v Mirza [2016] UKSC 42.

In support of a claimant's position, some potential arguments are as follows:

- An e-scooter rider's failure to comply with regulatory laws is usually not causative of the accident in question;

- There does not appear to be any case law that suggests that the driver of an uninsured or unregistered car cannot recover damages for replacement/repair (save in claims against the Motor Insurer's Bureau under the Uninsured Drivers' Agreements);

- There does not appear to be any case law that suggests an unlicenced driver cannot recover damages for replacement/repair;

- E-scooters can be ridden legitimately on private land and are available to purchase – they are not inherently illegal;

- It is impossible to insure or plate a privately owned e-scooter, yet e-scooters can be purchased legitimately. Therefore consumers are put in a difficult position. Their culpability/turpitude is minimal;

- As a matter of policy, most police authorities in England & Wales do not charge the riders of e-scooters with a criminal offence, save in the context of anti-social or dangerous use;

- Usually, a claimant is open and transparent about their use of an e-scooter. This can be contrasted with drivers who deliberatively avoid purchasing third-party insurance;

- Often, e-scooter riders are ignorant of the law. Although this is not a barrier to an illegality defence, it does potentially reduce any culpability or turpitude.

- Subject to the content of the new Transport Bill, legalisation of e-scooters on the road is imminent. It is very unlikely that third-party insurance, plating or driving licences will be required. In these circumstances, it is possible that a court may find that to debar a claim – even in part – would be disproportionate.

Conversely, the defendant is likely to raise the following:

- In nearly all cases, a claimant will be admitting (expressly or implicitly) to having committed several crimes;

- In many cases, such crimes are unlikely to have been an oversight. This is different to situations, for example, where an insurance policy expires without a driver's knowledge;

- The use of an e-scooter might be considered indicative of a wider anti-social approach on the part of a claimant, or even a wider lack of responsibility to other road users;

- It is widely reported in the media that e-scooters are not to be used on public roads;

- A claimant may have been riding in an aggressive or anti-social manner, increasing their culpability;

- A claimant may have been riding a particularly overpowered or fast e-scooter, increasing their culpability;

- There may be strong evidence that suggests that any repaired or replacement e-scooter would be ridden illegally.

These issues are novel and it is very unclear which arguments the Courts will favour. The author suspects that the Courts might be reluctant to penalise otherwise legitimate claimants for riding vehicles that are about to be legalised, but this is by no means certain.

## Contributory negligence

While illegal riding does not debar a claimant from bringing a claim, it might expose the rider to a finding of contributory negligence as long as the defendant can demonstrate that it was something about the vehicle or the way that it was ridden that *caused* the accident.

In the case of a micromobility device or e-scooter, a rider will not be contributorily negligent just for riding it in a road. After all, such vehicles can (in theory at least) be ridden on the road if plated and insured or if provided through a rental service. To find someone contributorily negligent in this situation would be akin to finding a driver of a car contributorily negligent in the case of an accident simply for not having insurance.

That said, press reports and the government's own investigations seem to suggest that there is a high incidence of antisocial, dangerous and careless riding on the part of e-scooter riders. If someone is already riding illegally there is no real incentive to ride well.

In the absence of guidance as to *how* to safely ride an e-scooter, the assumption has been that riders should be expected to follow a similar approach to cyclists. Rules 59 to 82 of the Highway Code set out specific rules for cyclists, some of which can easily be followed by e-scooter riders. For example, riders should not ride on the pavement and should also position themselves safely in the carriageway. Some of the rules are less easy for e-scooter riders to follow; for example the provision of rear lights on an e-scooter is not always feasible.

The effect of the Electric Scooter Trials and Traffic Signs (Coronavirus) Regulations and General Directions 2020 is that rental e-scooters can be ridden in similar places to bicycles and e-bikes. Scooters can be used on the road (except motorways) and in cycle lanes. They cannot be ridden on the pavement. Signs allowing and disallowing cycles will apply to e-scooter riders. It is arguable that a privately owned e-scooter rider also ought to follow these rules.

When considering whether a rider is contributorily negligent and to what extent, the Court is likely to consider the provisions of the Regulations and the Highway Code in relation to cyclists. It is likely that much of the case law regarding the negligence of cyclists or motorcyclists would apply to accidents involving riders of e-scooters. However, there are many differences between e-scooters and bikes and there may be some arguments that Courts should depart from the cycling case law. Some example arguments are:

- As many e-scooters are ridden illegally, there may be an assumption that a driver would not necessarily expect to see one in their path. This may make riders more blameworthy;

- The rapid acceleration of some e-scooters might mean that users will have to be more careful than a cyclist when setting off;

- E-scooters have smaller wheels and may not be as manoeuvrable as a bicycle or motorcycle on rough ground;

- E-scooters are normally silent or very quiet and their riders will have to be aware that other road users may not hear them;

- E-scooters and their riders will have a higher centre of gravity and might be more vulnerable to knocks or falls;

- E-scooters may sit in a different level in the Highway Code's hierarchy of road users, when compared to cyclists;

- It is difficult, if not impossible, to mount a visible rear light onto an e-scooter;

- The power and acceleration of e-scooters can be far higher than bicycles or e-bikes. For example, if a rider's speed was causative of an accident and the e-scooter was powered at more than 250 or 500 watts, there is an argument that the rider should be found contributorily negligent.

Ultimately, the usual approach to negligence will apply – an e-scooter rider has a duty of care to other road users and that duty requires them to ride with reasonable care and skill.

## *Helmets*

Helmets are not a legal requirement for riders of rental e-scooters. However, the assumption remains that by not using one when riding an e-scooter of any sort, a rider is putting themselves at risk.

The starting point for allegations of contributory negligence for failing to wear a helmet is Smith v Finch [2009] EWHC 53 (QB) which concerns cyclists and builds upon the case law in relation to seatbelts. Assuming that an e-scooter rider is travelling in an otherwise safe manner, the approach to contributory negligence for failing to wear a helmet is likely to the same as for a cyclist. However, there are arguments that due to the vulnerable road position of an e-scooter rider and the fast acceleration of such devices, a rider might be more blameworthy for failing to wear a helmet. These arguments have yet to be tested in the higher courts.

Helmets create a problem for the users of rental e-scooters. When renting an e-scooter, it is usually impossible to also rent a helmet alongside it. It is very unlikely that someone will bring a helmet with them on the off chance they might rent a scooter; the result is an uneasy understanding whereby the rental companies provide stark warnings to their customers to use helmets but provide no practical means of obtaining them. A rider might be considered less blameworthy for not wearing a helmet when no such helmets are available to them, although this principle does not yet appear to have been considered in any reported judgments.

## *Public liability*

There is a potential for claims to be brought by e-scooter riders against highways authorities for accidents caused by potholes and road surface defects under section 41 of the Highways Act 1980. There may also be claims under the Occupiers' Liability Act when an accident occurs on private land.

E-scooters and other micromobility devices tend to have small wheels that can more easily become caught in defects and potholes compared to bicycles or other vehicles. A small dip or defect that might be safe for bicycles or pedestrians could be very dangerous to an e-scooter rider, particularly when one considers the standing position of the rider and the relative speed of the vehicle.

The question then arises as to whether highways authorities are under a duty to consider the use of e-scooters when drafting policies for inspection and maintenance of road surfaces.

Again, there appears to be no law on this subject at present. It could be argued that where there is known to be a large volume of e-scooter users – for example where there is a well-used rental scheme in place – the authority responsible for the highway ought to consider this within their policies and provide a more rigorous system of inspection and maintenance. Conversely, it could be argued that until such time that private e-scooters are legal and used in sufficient numbers, it would not be reasonable to adopt a stricter approach to maintenance affording the authority a valid defence under section 58(2) of the Highways Act 1980.

## Claims under the Uninsured Drivers' Agreement

Prior to 2015, claimants under the Uninsured Drivers' Agreements would not be able to successfully recover damages from the MIB where:

> *'at the time of the use giving rise to the relevant liability [the claimant] was voluntarily allowing himself to be carried in the vehicle and, either before the commencement of his journey in the vehicle or after such commencement if he could reasonably be expected to have alighted from it, knew or ought to have known that... the vehicle was being used in the course or furtherance of a crime.'*

In the case of Delaney v Secretary of State for Transport [2014] EWHC 1785 (QB) this provision was found to be in breach of European law. Subsequently the clause was removed in the updated version of the Agreement. The effect is that the MIB cannot deny recovery to all privately-owned e-scooter users as a matter of course.

However, claims for the cost of repairing or replacing privately-owned e-scooters damaged in accidents will fail. This is because pursuant to clause 7(1) of the Uninsured Driver's Agreement 2015, drivers of uninsured vehicles who knew or ought to have known their vehicle was uninsured cannot make claims for vehicle damage. For the reasons stated above, e-scooters are 'motor vehicles' in law and they are unlikely to be insured. It is arguable that most claimants will be deemed to '*know or have reason to believe*' that this was the case.

## Personal accident insurance

If a rider of a rental e-scooter is injured, it is possible that they will be the beneficiary of an insurance policy as part of their fees. For example, Lime Micromobility – which provides rental e-scooters in London and elsewhere – has a deal with Allianz which will insure riders for their own bodily injuries, even if such injuries are the result of the rider themselves. Such insurance is also likely to include legal expenses. Accordingly, there may be arguments as to who will represent them in a claim for injury.

## Procedural issues

For the most part, claims by e-scooter riders will proceed as any other road traffic accident claim.

Claimants ought to note though that although e-scooter and micromobility device users are vulnerable on the road, they are not explicitly excluded from the Pre-Action Protocol for Personal Injury Claims below the Small Claims Limit in Road Traffic Accidents (also known as the RTA Small Claims Protocol).

The RTA Small Claims Protocol was introduced in 2021 and designed to create a streamlined system for dealing with low value whiplash cases involving occupants of motor vehicles. As a result, vulnerable road users such as pedestrians, motorcyclists, cyclists and horse riders are specifically excluded from the Protocol at paragraph 37. E-scooter riders and the users of other micromobility devices are not explicitly excluded. It remains unclear whether the courts will interpret this paragraph broadly and consider such riders (along with skateboarders and the riders of kick scooters) as vulnerable road users.

# Claims Against E-Scooter Riders

## Claims against insurers

Further to some well-publicised examples, it is now clear that an e-scooter rider can cause injury to pedestrians, cyclists and even cause damage to motor vehicles. Despite this, claims against e-scooter riders are low in number. The primary reason seems to be that the potential for e-scooters to cause injury and loss is relatively low.

However, the main impediment appears to be a misapprehension that e-scooter riders are uninsured or persons without means and that it is not financially viable to bring claims against them.

When it comes to rental e-scooters, the rider will be the beneficiary of third-party insurance provided as part of the rental payment. In those situations a claimant has a viable claim by recovering against the insurer.

The claim remains one against the rider of the e-scooter. If the rider is unknown, this creates difficulties for the claimant in a situation comparable to that in Cameron v Liverpool Victoria Insurance [2019] UKSC 6. Fortunately, riders of rental e-scooters are registered and tracked by GPS; if the rider is unknown it might be as simple as contacting the rental company for third-party disclosure. The name of the insurer can easily be ascertained by asking the rental company, or even looking at their website. For example, Lime Micromobility advertises that is insured by Allianz and Dott e-scooters in London are insured through a broker called Zego.

In practice, these claims will be treated like any other motor insurance claim against a driver and/or insurer.

## Claims against the MIB

When it comes to claims against the riders of private e-scooters or micromobility devices there is a very clear and valid path to recovery by bringing a claim against the MIB.

The MIB is an organisation funded by motor insurance. The purpose of the organisation is to help compensate victims of uninsured or untraced drivers of motor vehicles who would otherwise remain uncompensated. The framework for such claims is established in domestic and European law and implemented by way of the Uninsured Drivers' Agreement and the Untraced Drivers' Agreement, both most recently updated in 2017. Both of these Agreements adopt the definitions of 'motor vehicle' as set out in the Road Traffic Act 1988.

The case law as set out above suggests that micromobility devices are 'motor vehicles' for the purposes of the Road Traffic Act 1988 and therefore require a policy of insurance when ridden in public. It follows therefore, that if they are not insured and the rider causes an accident, liability to pay damages falls under the remit of the MIB.

Accordingly, if a pedestrian is struck and injured by a private e-scooter on the street, she ought to direct her claim against the MIB.

This usage of the MIB was not intended and means that, in effect, motorists and motorcyclists are paying to insure e-scooter riders. The introduction of (arguably vague) EU directives in 2013 and 2014 led to the potential legalisation of e-scooters throughout the EU with different jurisdictions offering vastly different laws and regulations regarding the insurance of such vehicles. The United Kingdom, however, did not change its position.

In August 2020, the MIB gave a statement to the Mail on Sunday as to their position. It could not be clearer:

> *"The government's failure to implement relevant EU law since 2014 has left the MIB bearing the costs for compensating victims who are hit by e-scooters. These claims are effectively funded by premium paying motorists and result – completely unfairly – in increased motor insurance premiums for all decent road users. This situation continues after the transition period ends, as this EU law requirement remains in UK law until the government legislates to remove it. So far, they have not committed to doing so."*

Whatever the views of the MIB and the insurance industry in general, the MIB remains the appropriate compensator in cases involving accidents caused by the riders of privately-owned e-scooters and other micromobility devices.

## Off-road Use

A series of recent European and domestic cases emerged over the last few years that dramatically expanded the definition of 'use of a motor vehicle' and the need for insurance. The 2016 Slovenian case of Vnuk v Zavarovalinca Triglav dd (C162/13) and the English cases of MIB v Lewis [2019] EWCA Civ 909, Pilling v UK Insurance [2017] EWCA Civ 259 and Lewington v MIB [2017] EWHC 2848 (Comm) established that as long as an accident was caused by the *'use of a motor vehicle'*, the motor insurer is liable, even if the use occurs off-road or on private land.

What emerged at the time was a dramatic expansion in the circumstances in which an insurer or the MIB was liable to compensate. As long as the accident iwass caused by the *use* of the vehicle, it did not matter where the accident took place.

With that in mind, it became easy to foresee the possibility of all sorts of injury claims involving e-scooters and micromobility devices being brought, even if they occurred on private land. For example, if a child rode his hoverboard into a sibling and caused an injury, the MIB could be a viable defendant even if the accident happened in a private garden. If an e-scooter battery exploded at home causing injury, it might also be said to arise from the 'use' of the vehicle and be the subject of a claim against the MIB.

The floodgates were opened.

However, this potential path has recently been closed by the Motor Vehicles (Compulsory Insurance) Act 2022 which creates a new section 156A of the Road Traffic Act 1988. The effect of the legislation is to remove the need for compulsory insurance *'otherwise than on a road or public place'*. Such legislation has been enabled by the UK leaving the European Union and marks a clear departure from established European law. It is notable that the European Commission has also proposed a partial departure from Vnuk.

The Act came into force on the 28th of June 2022 and is not retrospective. This means that any claims for prior accidents on private land can be diverted towards the MIB.

# Claims Against Rental Companies

## Negligence

It follows that if the rider of a rental e-scooter negligently causes an accident, it is the rider who is liable and not the rental company itself. They would bear no more culpability than (e.g.) Hertz or Avis for an accident involving a hire car.

However, there may be circumstances when it is appropriate to bring a claim involving a rental company, for example if the accident was caused by the negligent failure to maintain an e-scooter. There may also be circumstances where the rental company, by virtue of its own failings, caused or permitted someone inappropriate to ride a scooter and subsequently caused an accident. These types of claims will be rare, fact-specific and difficult to prosecute.

Possible sources of claims are those caused by geofencing. Geofencing is a process whereby e-scooters (or indeed e-bikes) are prevented by way of GPS from being used outside a designated area as if bound by an imaginary fence. When the vehicle is taken outside the geofenced area, the motor ceases. This prevents the scooters from being easily taken away from where they are required or where they cannot be rented in accordance with their rental company's licence. There have been examples of e-scooters unexpectedly stopping at a geofence, with the sudden loss of momentum causing riders to fall and injure themselves. The author's experience of geofencing is that when taken out of the area, deceleration is slow and the risk of injury is very low. Although geofencing accidents remain a possibility, the actions of rental companies to reduce the risk have been substantial and such claims seem unlikely to succeed.

## Public liability

One big concern of many campaigners against rental e-scooters has been the potential nuisance caused by dock-less e-scooters blocking the footway. Such scooters present obvious tripping hazards, particularly to the blind and partially sighted.

If someone is injured in this manner, liability is likely to be decided on matters of public policy. The risks of pedestrians will have to be weighed against the policy decision to have e-scooters conveniently available throughout a city. It seems unlikely that a court would find a rental company negligent if the decision to have a dock-less system if the system has been approved and licenced by a local council. It is also notable that many e-scooter providers incentivise users to drop their scooters in designated areas, limiting the tripping risk to pedestrians. The author suspects that claimants will find it difficult to succeed in these circumstances.

# Future Trends

## An unsatisfactory position

The situation with regard to privately-owned e-scooters and micromobility devices is plagued with a lack of clarity. The law is fairly unambiguous that their use is forbidden on roads and in public spaces but this is counterbalanced with an approach to enforcement that borders on tolerance.

It is difficult for road users and consumers to know where their obligations lie. An online search for e-scooters reveals a plethora of articles about the legality or illegality of such devices, much of it wrong or poorly considered.

Stakeholders from all sides are advocating for reform. Whilst a minority of voices are calling for an outright ban on safety grounds, the majority opinion seems to be that the use of e-scooters and micromobility devices ought to be legalised but robustly regulated. This appears to be the view of the Government, who have announced that it is their intention to legalise e-scooters.

Whatever approach is taken, it seems that the law on e-scooter and micromobility use is very likely to change in the coming years.

## Results of the e-scooter trial

As of the time of publication, the Trial has been extended to November 2022 and it remains uncertain what the results will be. In January 2022, it was suggested that an interim report dealing with the monitoring and evaluation of the Trial would be published in Spring 2022 with a final report at the end of 2022. As of the date of writing in July 2022, neither of these are available.

Nevertheless, despite the ongoing trials, the Government in May 2022 announced that as part of the current Parliament, a Transport Bill will be introduced which will effectively legalise and regulate the use of e-scooters. It would appear that the Government has judged the trials to be a success and has expedited legislation before the trial has even concluded.

## A call for a ban

It is safe to say that there is a large selection of the population who do not wish to see e-scooters legalised. The primary motivator seems to be one of safety. The Government's own figures[3] for the year ending June 2021 suggests 931 people injured in accidents involving e-scooters, including three deaths. The vast majority of those injured were the riders themselves, although a small number of pedestrians, cyclists and motorcyclists appear to have been hurt in collisions with e-scooters. Later figures presented to Parliament suggest that 11 deaths were caused by the use of private e-scooters in 2021. These numbers are relatively small in comparison with those injured in motoring or cycling accidents, but this is likely a reflection of the low but growing number of e-scooter riders.

The majority of riders injured appear to be males under 30, which is unsurprising. The demographics of riders appear to be young, male and urban. Despite only 21.8% of road traffic accidents in Great Britain being reported to the Metropolitan Police in London, over 53% of e-scooter collisions fell under their jurisdiction. The result is a

[3] 'Reported road casualties Great Britain: e-scooter factsheet year ending June 2021. https://www.gov.uk/government/statistics/reported-road-casualties-great-britain-e-scooter-factsheet-year-ending-june-2021/reported-road-casualties-great-britain-e-scooter-factsheet-year-ending-june-2021

demographic – and perhaps even a political – divide between those that are in favour of e-scooters and those that regard them as a menace.

This approach is reflected in the press. Readers will be familiar with newspaper articles emphasising the dangers of e-scooter use.

Disabled, and in particular blind/partially sighted pedestrians, appear to be particularly vulnerable. Some disability advocacy groups also have called for an outright ban.

In the only parliamentary debate on the topic, the House of Lords heard arguments in January 2022. Several Conservative Lords called for an outright ban on e-scooters on safety grounds, drawing upon their own experiences as pedestrians, and in several cases as disabled persons. Arguably, the demographic make-up of the Lords does not reflect the typical e-scooter user, leading to a largely one-sided debate.

In response, the Baroness Vere of Norbiton, speaking on behalf of the Department for Transport put forward a more nuanced view:

> *"… the Government believe that, with the right regulations, there is potential for significant economic, social and environmental benefits from light, zero-emission vehicles such as e-scooters… We want a safe, proportionate and flexible regulatory framework if we decide that is our way forward. We have been gathering plenty of evidence: we have responses to the future of transport regulatory review, and there is further stakeholder engagement to do, including state engagement with the insurance industry. No decision has been taken about the future legal status of e-scooters."*

Notwithstanding the views of those calling for a ban, the Government seem very keen to press on and regulate e-scooter use, even before the final results of the e-scooter pilot are published.

## Pro-legalisation voices

The public and individual benefits of e-scooter use are numerous:

- Being electric, e-scooters are emission-free at the point of use and are generally far more efficient and far less polluting than vehicles with internal combustion engines. This assists with both local air quality and global carbon emissions.

- They are small and portable in a way that bicycles and other vehicles are not, making them more convenient than many other forms of transport.

- They require little physical effort to use, making them viable to many with disabilities who would not, for example, be able to ride a bicycle.

- They are extremely cheap to purchase and run in comparison with other motor vehicles and are accessible to those on low incomes. At a time of high living costs and high inflation, this is of particular importance.

- They do not require public transport infrastructure and therefore are of particular benefit to those in areas with poor existing infrastructure.

- If users were to switch from other modes of transport, the result could be a decrease in traffic or congestion.

- As a form of individual transport, they can reduce the potential spread of viruses. This was of particular importance during the Covid-19 pandemic.

One important stakeholder is the Association of British Insurers (the ABI), which in March 2022 called for the introduction of an effective regulatory system that strikes *'the right balance between ensuring public safety on the one hand and encouraging innovative approaches to transport on the other'.* The ABI calls for coherent standards in respect of construction, and certainty as to where and how e-scooters can be used. Perhaps most importantly, they ask that no liability falls on the MIB for accidents caused by the riders of e-scooters without some sort of contribution from riders in the form of mandatory third-party insurance.

The Government has published two summary reports that give an indication as to where legislation and legalisation may head. Both deal with public perceptions of e-scooter use and were published in the height of the Covid-19 pandemic. Interestingly, although the reports give both pro and anti-legalisation stances, the conclusions seem to be that in terms of public opinion, *'there was widespread agreement that e-scooters should be legalised and regulated'*[4].

## The Transport Bill

In April 2022 in advance of the Government setting out its legislative agenda, the Transport Secretary told the House of Commons Transport Committee that there were plans to introduce legislation to regulate e-scooters. In May 2022, as part of the Queen's Speech, it was announced that the Government intended to introduce legislation to regulate the use of privately-owned e-scooters as part of the 2022/2023 legislative session.

[4] Public Attitudes to the Use of E-scooters in the UK, Department for Transport, Nov 2020. Amy Busby, Samantha Bond, Lauren Wiginton, Lucy Williams.

At the time of publication, detail of any proposed legislation is scant.

The plan appears to be to set out clear regulatory standards for e-scooters which should '*stipulate that all e-scooters sold met certain standards concerning speed, power and lights, among other things*'.

Given the issues as set out above, there remains disquiet on the backbenches of the Conservative Party and it is unclear whether such legislation will pass and in what form. In his address to the Transport Committee setting out the Government's plans, the Transport Secretary was immediately questioned by a member of his own party regarding the safety of e-scooters in general,

On the face of it, the legislation is likely to be modelled on the Electrically Assisted Pedal Cycles Regulations 1983 (the regulations that govern the use of e-bikes – see below), with e-scooters being designated a specific type of vehicle and exempt from the regulatory hurdles that come with being considered a 'motor vehicle' for the purposes of the Road Traffic Act 1988. Baroness Vere told the Lords:

> *"... if they are to be legalised, we would consider removing them from the motor vehicle category and instead creating a new bespoke category of vehicles with the appropriate regulatory regime in place."*

It is likely that the legal requirements for e-scooters will broadly follow that of rental scooters:

## *Power and speed*

It is notable that although e-bikes are limited to 250 watts of power output, existing rental e-scooters are allowed to have double the power at 500 watts. This seems somewhat inconsistent, although this extra provision for power could account for the fact that rental scooters are heavier as they have to carry large batteries for longer period of use between charges. Arguably, privately-owned e-scooters do not have to carry these large batteries and so a 250-watt limit may be appropriate, bringing the power limit in line with e-bikes. Whether the Regulations say 500 watts or 250 watts, there will be an inconsistency of approach.

Looking at what is available to purchase, e-scooters seem to be available with anything from 120 watts to 8000 watts of power. Post-legalisation, it is likely that many previously purchased vehicles will not be compliant with the legislation.

Current e-bikes and rental e-scooters are limited to 15.5mph. This is higher than some other jurisdictions. In Berlin, for example, these are limited to 12.5mph. It is lower than Barcelona, where e-scooters can travel on roads at up to 18.6mph[5].

On balance, it seems very unlikely that the Government will depart from the existing 15.5mph limit. However, a DfT report seems to suggest that the general public consensus for a maximum speed limit would be 20mph[6].

## *Form, shape, size and design*

It seems very likely that only e-scooters that comply with a very specific form-factor will be legalised. Presumably these will be stand-up scooters with handlebars as allowed for within the Trials. Arguably, weight limits could be reduced as larger batteries are not required if the scooter is for personal use.

---

[5] Future of Transport Regulatory Review: Modernising Vehicle Standards, Department for Transport, Sep 21

[6] Public Attitudes to the Use of E-scooters in the UK, Department for Transport, Nov 2020.

## *Construction and safety*

It is very likely as with all other powered vehicles, there is appropriate certification to ensure that the vehicle is safe. This may take the form of self-certification or by a type-approval process. This is particularly important for devices that rely upon the use of lithium-ion batteries that are susceptible to combustion. There are likely to be specific construction regulations, as with e-bikes.

One clear benefit to certification is that it will make it easier for police forces to check whether a particular vehicle is compliant with regulations.

## *Rider restrictions*

It is difficult to predict what the legislation will say in this regard. For example, will the Bill and any subsequent Regulations limit riders to being over 14 as with e-bikes? Will a driving licence be required? At this stage, it is too early to tell.

What does seem to be relatively clear is that as in the Trials, regulated e-scooters will be able to be used on roads, mixed-use paths and cycle paths but not on pavements.

## *Insurance*

The assumption going forward is that when it comes to e-scooters, the insurance position is likely to be similar to that of e-bikes with no requirement for third-party insurance. This would reduce the barriers of entry and limit the costs exposure to insurers and the MIB. If insurance is required, some sort of registration and database will also be necessary; the costs and regulatory hurdles of such a system would likely remove any practical benefit of using an e-scooter in the first place.

## *Conclusions*

As of the time of writing in June 2022, it appears to be very clear that legalisation and regulation is coming for some e-scooters. Whatever the wording of the proposed Bill, a detailed regulatory framework will provide clarity as to where, when and in what form factor micromobility devices can be used on public roads.

Assuming that this is accompanied by a public education campaign, guides for the police and the funds for enforcement, it is likely to be a success. Without these, the current confusion will remain.

Absent from much of the discussion regarding legalisation are micromobility devices that are not e-scooters. These do not form part of the trial and nor are there many voices calling for their legalisation.

The reality is that if a clear regulatory framework is introduced for e-scooters, these are likely to be in a prescribed form, with clear construction regulations set out, as with other methods of transport such as e-bikes. The result is that even if e-scooters are legalised, there will still remain a large number of vehicles, e-scooters and e-bikes that fall outside the scope of any regulations and remain 'motor vehicles' for the purposes of the Road Traffic Act 1988.

It is unclear whether the proposed Transport Bill will deal with these.

# PART TWO

# E-BIKES

# E-bikes and the Need for Regulation

An e-bike, e-cycle, electric bicycle or 'electrically assisted pedal cycle' to use the official term, is a pedal cycle with a small integrated motor which allows it to be propelled using electricity. When a rider starts pedalling, the motor provides electrical assistance, propelling the rider and the bike forward. Unlike a motorcycle, an e-bike cannot be propelled without pedal power.

The advantage of an e-bike over a normal pedal bike is that a cyclist can travel faster and further without expending as much energy. This is of benefit to those who would otherwise be unable to cycle, those who wish to cycle further and faster, and those who wish to travel without sweating or exerting themselves. Further advantages of an e-bike over a motorcycle are that it is lighter, cheaper and does not require a licence or insurance.

A more accurate term for these forms of transport might be 'e-cycle', which describes a wide class of electrically assisted pedal cycles including bicycles, tricycles, tandems and electric cargo bikes. However, for the purposes of simplicity, throughout this book I have used the common term 'e-bike' as a catch-all term for these cycles.

# The Electrically Assisted Pedal Cycles Regulations 1983

## Background

Although e-bikes are seen as a relatively new concept, they date back as far as the first half of the twentieth century. Early e-bikes were heavy, bulky and had very limited range. Throughout the twentieth century, where motorcycles existed, internal combustion engines represented a clear advantage to most riders. During the 1970s and the oil crisis, e-bikes developed a niche following in countries such as Germany and the Netherlands.

In the early 1980s the UK government, perhaps inspired by other countries in Europe, passed legislation that would allow the use of e-bikes on British roads: the Electrically Assisted Pedal Cycles Regulations 1983/1168 ("the EAPC Regulations"). The pressure to legislate appears to have come manufacturers who wished to enter the marketplace with new and innovative types of transport.

The thinking behind the EAPC Regulations is summarised in a speech given to the House of Lords by Lord Lucas of Chilworth[7]:

> *"... There has been a great deal of interest in, and support for, the proposals. Manufacturers have told us that there is a real market for such vehicles, and some have already received advance orders. The vehicle will be of particular help to the aged, handicapped and infirm, but will also benefit many people who simply want moderately priced, easy to use, inexpensive to operate and simple transport. The vehicles also*

[7] HL Deb 27 July 1983 vol 443 cc1605-6

> *provide something of a bonus from an environmental viewpoint, being essentially pollution-free."*

What was anticipated in 1983 was not necessarily an e-bike as we know it today. The Regulations were drafted broadly to allow electric tricycles and tandems, hoping that there would be innovation in the marketplace. One early hope for British e-cycles in the 1980s was the Sinclair C5, an electric tricycle in which the rider was seated in a recumbent position. Generally considered heavy, unwieldy and overly expensive, it was not a financial success. Indeed, despite the hopes of the Government and other stakeholders, battery and motor technology meant that a useful, commercially viable electric personal transport was out of reach until the 1990s.

## Effect of the Regulations

The purpose of the EAPC Regulations was to create a new class of electric vehicle that would be subject to its own regulation.

The mechanism adopted was to add e-bikes to a list of vehicle types which were not to be treated as motor vehicles for the purposes of section 103 of the Road Traffic Regulation Act 1967 and section 193 of the Road Traffic Act 1972. These have both since been replaced by section 140 of the Road Traffic Regulation Act 1984 and section 189 of the Road Traffic Act 1988 respectively.

The result of being added to this list was that e-bikes became exempt from many of the onerous regulatory requirements faced by motorcycle and moped riders, notably the need for insurance, registration and the wearing of a helmet. E-bike riders were now to be treated in a similar way to other cyclists and allowed to use cycleways and mixed-use paths.

The only substantive difference for riders is that section 32 of the Road Traffic Act 1988 creates a criminal offence for those who ride an e-bike under age fourteen or *'knowing or suspecting that another person is under the age of fourteen, causes or permits him to drive such a pedal cycle'.*

## Implementation

The EAPC Regulations came into force on the 12th of August 1983.

The Regulations have since been substantially amended by the Electrically Assisted Pedal Cycles (Amendment) Regulations 2015.

## Requirement 1: Weight Limit

There were three straightforward requirements that must be satisfied for an e-bike to be considered an EAPC under the Regulations.

The first of this is the weight limit, which is set out at Regulation 4(a).

Bicycles were subject to an unladen weight limit of 40kg. For tandems and tricycles the weight limit was 60kg. A tandem is defined as a bicycle designed to carry two or more persons at least two of whom can propel the vehicle. Feasibly, the Regulations would apply to a bicycle for three people.

It is notable that tricycles are included within the Regulations, meaning that vehicles such as the Sinclair C5 (see above) were made road-legal.

It is also notable that four-wheeled vehicles would not fall under the remit of the Regulations.

## Requirement 2: Pedals

Regulation 4(b) states that the vehicle shall be fitted with pedals by means of which it is capable of being propelled.

This is perhaps the most important defining feature of an e-bike and separates it from traditional powered bikes such as mopeds and motorcycles. Electric motorcycles do exist and are separately regulated alongside traditional motorcycles.

In Winter v DPP [2002] EWHC 1524 (Admin), the rider of a vehicle described as a "City Bug" was charged with the offence of driving without insurance contrary to s.143 of the Road Traffic Act 1988. The City Bug appears to have been an early electric tricycle. In pictures it resembles a modern mobility scooter. Ms Winter's defence was that the vehicle was exempt from the need for insurance as it was an EAPC for the purposes of the Regulations. The Crown successfully argued that the pedals attached to the City Bug were tiny in comparison to the vehicle and did not drive a chain, but turned the front wheel itself. On appeal by way of case stated, it was found that *'capable of being propelled'* by pedals was to be read as *'reasonably capable of being propelled'*. The judge made a finding of fact that the City Bug would not be a useful or safe conveyance if reliance was placed on pedals alone. Accordingly, it is not enough for an e-bike to have pedals – the cycle has to be capable of being used as a reasonable form of transport using pedal power alone.

## Requirement 3: Power and Speed Limits

Regulation 4(c)(i) limited the continuous rated output of a motor on a bicycle to 200 watts. For tandems and tricycles, the maximum was 250 watts.

Regulation 4(c)(ii) restricts the motor from propelling the e-bike when it is travelling at more than 15mph.

# The Electrically Assisted Pedal Cycles (Amendment) Regulations 2015

Technological improvements, including the development of the rechargeable lithium-ion battery and smaller, more powerful motors led from e-bikes transitioning from niche product to a mainstream form of technology in the 2000s. A modern form of electric bicycle emerged that required more modern regulation.

EU legislation[8] set out features of an EAPC that exempted it from approval at the manufacturing stage. The result was regulatory misalignment between the EU and the UK; an e-bike built in Germany might not meet the British criteria for an EAPC. Intervention was required to harmonise British regulations with the EU market and minimise the risk of barrier-to-trade legal challenges.

Interestingly, as part of the impact assessment when considering the regulations, there was a forecasted increase in e-bike sales from around 12,550 in 2014 to 20,400 in 2024. This was a significant underestimation of the growth of e-bikes; by 2018 the figure exceeded 50,000. Growth in the market is likely to have accelerated further since the start of the Covid-19 pandemic.

The Regulations came into force on the 6th of April 2015.

## *Requirement 1: Weight limit*

Changes in battery technology had meant the adoption of easily-rechargeable lithium-ion batteries, which tend to be significantly lighter than lead-acid batteries. The weight of modern e-bikes was

[8] Regulation 168/2013, Article 2(h)

thought to be no longer a safety issue and the weight requirement was removed.

## *Requirement 2: Pedals*

This is unaffected by the 2015 Regulations.

## *Requirement 3: Power and Speed Limits*

In 2009, CEN, the European Standards body set out a new standard for e-bikes. Under this standard, the power output for two-wheeled EAPCS was limited to 250 watts. The speed up to which the electric motor was to provide assistance was 25kph.

Regulation 168/2013 dealt with motorcycles generally. The Regulation specifically excluded EAPCs as long as the power did not exceed 250 watts and that the motor assistance *reduced progressively with speed* and cut out at 25kph. This progressive reduction was only possible as a result of newer motor and sensor technology that had since become an industry standard.

The net result was that compliant EAPCs manufactured within the EU could be too powerful and fast to be legal under British law. The 2015 Regulations therefore increased the maximum power to 250 watts and increased the relevant speed to 15.5mph, the imperial equivalent of 25kph.

## *Other changes*

The 2015 Regulations allow for e-bikes to have more than three wheels, allowing for the provision of quadricycles, 'bike cars', velomobiles and other similar vehicles.

# The Pedal Cycle (Construction and Use) Regulations

Regulations concerning the construction of e-bikes were introduced in 1983 and amended in 2015 in parallel with the EAPC Regulations.

The Pedal Cycle (Construction and Use) Regulations 1983, as amended by the Pedal Cycles (Construction and Use) (Amendment) Regulations 2015 set out specific standards for e-bikes. This specified that no person shall ride, or cause or permit to be ridden an EAPC unless the following apply:

- A plate showing the name of the manufacturer, voltage and 'continuous rated output' of the motor, or (for more modern e-bikes) the name of the manufacturer, maximum speed and maximum continuous rated power (reg 4(a));
- Braking systems that meet national standards (reg 4(b));
- Batteries 'that do not leak as to be a source of danger' (reg 4(c));
- A 'device biased to the off position' – meaning that the motor is only powered when the device is operated (reg 4(d)).

Regulation 4A refers back to EU Regulations for braking standards and construction requirements. One practical consequence of this new Regulation, added in 2015, is that bikes with 'walk-assist' or 'twist and go' throttles do not fit within these new standards.

If an e-bike does not meet the Regulations, for example it can be propelled without pedalling by way of a throttle, it will have to be Type Approved by the Driving and Vehicle Standards Agency (DVSA). Manufactures or individuals can apply for this. Anecdotally,

Type Approval can be very inconsistent, with applicants at the mercy of differing approaches by the DVSA.

Other construction regulations, such as those that apply to sale/supply and testing/inspection are the same as for non-electric bikes.

## Liability and Contributory Negligence

E-bikes are treated just as pedal cycles for the purposes of the law. There are few reported cases of accidents involving e-bikes and nothing to suggest that the courts will approach liability or contributory negligence any differently just because the bike is electrically assisted. Any case law that applies to the riding of a pedal bicycle is likely to equally apply to the riding of an e-bike, including the usage of protective helmets.

In the case of a non-compliant e-bike, there may be exceptions. For example, if a bike is adapted such that it can travel at an electrically assisted speed of more than 15.5mph and such speed is causative of an accident, there is an argument that the rider ought to be found contributorily negligent. In the absence of case law, it is unclear how the courts might approach issues of causative potency and blameworthiness.

# Speed Pedelecs

There are exceptions that allow more powerful or faster e-bikes to be ridden on the road. Such bikes are informally known as 'speed pedelecs' or 's-pedelecs'. These bikes are not compliant with the EAPC Regulations 2015 and are effectively mopeds for the purposes of the law. Speed pedelecs are best thought of as ad-hoc electric motorcycles with pedals.

As of the date of publication, there are no domestic or EU regulations that apply specifically to speed pedelecs.

As these bikes are considered mopeds, riders have an obligation to:

- Wear a helmet (Motor Cycles (Protective Helmets) Regulations 1998);
- Have third-party insurance (section 143, Road Traffic Act 1988);
- Have an appropriate driving licence (section 87, Road Traffic Act 1988);
- Obtain type approval from the DVSA;
- Register the vehicle with the Driver and Vehicle Licensing Agency (DVLA);
- Display a number plate;
- Obtain an MOT certificate;

Riders will also be required to observe speed limits (section 88) and will be unable to use cycle lanes (section 34 of the Road Traffic Act 1988).

It is rare to see a plated, insured bicycle. The process for registering a bicycle with the DVLA and then obtaining insurance upon it is considered to be very difficult. For now, speed pedelecs are generally used only by hobbyists with an overlapping knowledge of cycle engineering, the DVSA, the DVLA and the insurance industry.

# Non-Compliant E-Bikes

E-bikes that do not meet the 1983 Regulations (as amended) are considered motor vehicles for the purposes of section 189 of the Road Traffic Act 1988.

As motor vehicles, the rider will be expected to insure and plate their vehicle and have a driving licence if ridden on the road. In practice, this is likely to be impossible. Unless the bike meets the onerous regulatory criteria to be a legal speed pedelec, it will probably be considered a non-type-approved motorcycle for the purposes of the law.

For insurance purposes and for the purposes of the criminal law, there is a significant distinction between a compliant and non-compliant e-bike.

Non-compliant bikes are increasingly common and are usually imported, created or adapted to meet the needs of enthusiasts or delivery riders. Enforcement can be poor as police forces often do not have the funding, the will nor the knowledge to assess whether a particular bike is compliant. From a practical perspective, non-compliant bikes can often be spotted by:

- Obviously travelling at speeds in excess of 15.5mph;
- Moving without the rider using the pedals;
- The use of a throttle for acceleration;
- Obvious modifications, extra wiring or the use of gaffer tape;
- A lack of a plate/sticker on the frame from the manufacturer indicating compliance.

Mainstream and high street retailers tend to only stock e-bikes that are compliant. However, cheaper models, usually Chinese bikes imported on the grey market, tend to be non-compliant.

As different jurisdictions have different power and speed limits, e-bikes are often sold in a standardised form for international markets, albeit with software-based speed limitations for UK and European markets that have more restrictive laws. There are examples of bikes that can be 'chipped', overridden or simply programmed to go faster. There is one well-publicised example of a Dutch e-bike controlled by a phone app; European users could simply tell the app that they were in the United States and would immediately see their maximum pedal-assisted speed rise to 20mph.

The result is that a surprisingly large proportion of e-bikes on British roads do not comply with the EAPC Regulations. In these circumstances, it is possible that if a rider of a non-compliant e-bike is injured in an accident, a defendant may refuse to compensate them on grounds of illegality. I have dealt with this issue above in the chapter on *ex turpi causa* arguments in the context of e-scooters.

# Insurance

The effect of s189(1)(c) of the Road Traffic Act 1988 is that e-bikes that fall under the remit of the EAPC Regulations are not considered motor vehicles. From a regulatory perspective, they operate as if they are normal pedal cycles. From an insurance liability perspective, this means that third-party insurance is not required. If a rider causes an accident they will be personally liable for any loss, but any recovery will be limited to what a victim can recover from the rider personally.

If an e-bike is not compliant with the Regulations, it is considered a motor vehicle and therefore ought to be insured. In the absence of insurance, the MIB will be an appropriate source of compensation (see the chapters above in relation to claims against the MIB for e-scooter accidents). It is therefore very important that if the rider of an e-bike causes an accident, any potential victims seek disclosure of compliance with the EAPC Regulations and witnesses are asked to describe the appearance and riding style of the bike. In the absence of compliance, a claim for injury and loss may suddenly become viable as there will now be a funder in place.

It is ironic that the victims of accidents are likely to be better off if the accident was caused by someone riding a non-compliant bike.

# Delivery Riders

Delivery riders, such as those delivering takeaway food represent a large proportion of e-bike riders. From a legal perspective they present their own challenges, particularly if they are involved in an accident.

If a person is struck by a delivery rider, the appropriate person against whom to claim is the rider himself rather than the delivery company. Although there is the possibility of widening vicarious liability to those within the gig economy (see the judgment of Lady Hale in Barclays Bank v Various Claimants [2020] UKSC 13), things are different when it comes to road traffic accidents. Here it is all about the allocation of financial risk. Motorcycle riders and car-based delivery drivers will be expected to have their own motor insurance for these events. In the context of bikes and e-bikes, there is no obligation to have any third-party insurance at all.

Nevertheless, from a practical perspective it may be useful for a claimant to contact the delivery company to provide details of the rider, the route taken and any insurance they or their rider may have. This may be fruitful – for example, Deliveroo provide third-party insurance to their cycle delivery riders and this appears to extend to the riders of e-bikes as well.

Anecdotally, delivery riders are more likely than riders in general to ride e-bikes that are not compliant with the EAPC Regulations. This might be because there are incentives to travel at speed and with minimum effort in order to increase the number of deliveries made, and therefore income received. In this situation, any third-party insurance is likely to be void and a claim should be made against the MIB under the Uninsured Drivers' Agreement as set out above.

If a delivery rider is injured, for example if they are struck by a car, any issues as to liability are likely to be the same as for a pedal cyclists. The main issues likely to arise are those relating to *ex turpi causa* and the recoverability of the cost of repairs/replacement e-bike. I have dealt with these arguments above in the context of e-scooters.

## Criminal Penalties

The criminal offences committed by the rider of a non-compliant e-bike are likely to be similar to those of the rider of a privately-owned e-scooter. Charges are likely to take the form of a Fixed Penalty Notice. Non-compliant bikes are also liable to seizure. I have dealt with this above in the context of e-scooters.

# The Future

Despite many voices calling for reform of the law when it comes to e-scooters and micromobility devices, there are few calling for changes to the EAPC Regulations. They have been in place for nearly 40 years and are generally considered fit for purpose, allowing for clear standards and the importation of e-bikes built for the European market.

One potential area of reform is in regard to speed and power limits, which by international standards are very low. For example, in most US states the maximum speed limit is 20mph. Many states allow a maximum power output of 1000 watts, which is four times higher than in the UK or EU. 15.5mph is not particularly fast, especially when compared to the speed of many road cyclists travelling on their own pedal power.

It remains to be seen whether the arbitrary limits from 1983 and 2015 will remain viable as electric cycling evolves from a niche hobby to a mainstream form of travel.

For now, the law remains established, clear and simple. In the absence of any new technologies or an intention to depart from European law, the law in relation to e-bikes is unlikely to change significantly in the future.

| |
|---|
| 'A Practical Guide to the EU Succession Regulation' by Richard Frimston |
| 'A Practical Guide to Solicitor and Client Costs – 2nd Edition' by Robin Dunne |
| 'Constructive Dismissal – Practice Pointers and Principles' by Benjimin Burgher |
| 'A Practical Guide to Religion and Belief Discrimination Claims in the Workplace' by Kashif Ali |
| 'A Practical Guide to the Law of Medical Treatment Decisions' by Ben Troke |
| 'Fundamental Dishonesty and QOCS in Personal Injury Proceedings: Law and Practice' by Jake Rowley |
| 'A Practical Guide to the Law in Relation to School Exclusions' by Charlotte Hadfield & Alice de Coverley |
| 'A Practical Guide to Divorce for the Silver Separators' by Karin Walker |
| 'The Right to be Forgotten – The Law and Practical Issues' by Melissa Stock |
| 'A Practical Guide to Planning Law and Rights of Way in National Parks, the Broads and AONBs' by James Maurici QC, James Neill et al |
| 'A Practical Guide to Election Law' by Tom Tabori |
| 'A Practical Guide to the Law in Relation to Surrogacy' by Andrew Powell |
| 'A Practical Guide to Claims Arising from Fatal Accidents – 2nd Edition' by James Patience |
| 'A Practical Guide to the Ownership of Employee Inventions – From Entitlement to Compensation' by James Tumbridge & Ashley Roughton |
| 'A Practical Guide to Asbestos Claims' by Jonathan Owen & Gareth McAloon |
| 'A Practical Guide to Stamp Duty Land Tax in England and Northern Ireland' by Suzanne O'Hara |
| 'A Practical Guide to the Law of Farming Partnerships' by Philip Whitcomb |
| 'Covid-19, Homeworking and the Law – The Essential Guide to Employment and GDPR Issues' by Forbes Solicitors |
| 'Covid-19 and Criminal Law – The Essential Guide' by Ramya Nagesh |
| 'Covid-19 and Family Law in England and Wales – The Essential Guide' by Safda Mahmood |
| 'A Practical Guide to the Law of Unlawful Eviction and Harassment – 2nd Edition' by Stephanie Lovegrove |
| 'Covid-19, Brexit and the Law of Commercial Leases – The Essential Guide' by Mark Shelton |
| 'A Practical Guide to Costs in Personal Injury Claims – 2nd Edition' by Matthew Hoe |

| |
|---|
| 'A Practical Guide to the General Data Protection Regulation (GDPR) – 2nd Edition' by Keith Markham |
| 'Ellis on Credit Hire – Sixth Edition' by Aidan Ellis & Tim Kevan |
| 'A Practical Guide to Working with Litigants in Person and McKenzie Friends in Family Cases' by Stuart Barlow |
| 'Protecting Unregistered Brands: A Practical Guide to the Law of Passing Off' by Lorna Brazell |
| 'A Practical Guide to Secondary Liability and Joint Enterprise Post-Jogee' by Joanne Cecil & James Mehigan |
| 'A Practical Guide to the Pre-Action RTA Claims Protocol for Personal Injury Lawyers' by Antonia Ford |
| 'A Practical Guide to Neighbour Disputes and the Law' by Alexander Walsh |
| 'A Practical Guide to Forfeiture of Leases' by Mark Shelton |
| 'A Practical Guide to Coercive Control for Legal Practitioners and Victims' by Rachel Horman |
| 'A Practical Guide to Rights Over Airspace and Subsoil' by Daniel Gatty |
| 'Tackling Disclosure in the Criminal Courts – A Practitioner's Guide' by Narita Bahra QC & Don Ramble |
| 'A Practical Guide to the Law of Driverless Cars – Second Edition' by Alex Glassbrook, Emma Northey & Scarlett Milligan |
| 'A Practical Guide to TOLATA Claims' by Greg Williams |
| 'A Practical Guide to Elderly Law – 2nd Edition' by Justin Patten |
| 'A Practical Guide to Responding to Housing Disrepair and Unfitness Claims' by Iain Wightwick |
| 'A Practical Guide to the Construction and Rectification of Wills and Trust Instruments' by Edward Hewitt |
| 'A Practical Guide to the Law of Bullying and Harassment in the Workplace' by Philip Hyland |
| 'How to Be a Freelance Solicitor: A Practical Guide to the SRA-Regulated Freelance Solicitor Model' by Paul Bennett |
| 'A Practical Guide to Prison Injury Claims' by Malcolm Johnson |
| 'A Practical Guide to the Small Claims Track - 2nd Edition' by Dominic Bright |
| 'A Practical Guide to Advising Clients at the Police Station' by Colin Stephen McKeown-Beaumont |
| 'A Practical Guide to Antisocial Behaviour Injunctions' by Iain Wightwick |

| |
|---|
| 'Practical Mediation: A Guide for Mediators, Advocates, Advisers, Lawyers, and Students in Civil, Commercial, Business, Property, Workplace, and Employment Cases' by Jonathan Dingle with John Sephton |
| 'The Mini-Pupillage Workbook' by David Boyle |
| 'A Practical Guide to Crofting Law' by Brian Inkster |
| 'A Practical Guide to Spousal Maintenance' by Liz Cowell |
| 'A Practical Guide to the Law of Domain Names and Cybersquatting' by Andrew Clemson |
| 'A Practical Guide to the Law of Gender Pay Gap Reporting' by Harini Iyengar |
| 'A Practical Guide to the Rights of Grandparents in Children Proceedings' by Stuart Barlow |
| 'NHS Whistleblowing and the Law' by Joseph England |
| 'Employment Law and the Gig Economy' by Nigel Mackay & Annie Powell |
| 'A Practical Guide to Noise Induced Hearing Loss (NIHL) Claims' by Andrew Mckie, Ian Skeate, Gareth McAloon |
| 'An Introduction to Beauty Negligence Claims – A Practical Guide for the Personal Injury Practitioner' by Greg Almond |
| 'Intercompany Agreements for Transfer Pricing Compliance' by Paul Sutton |
| 'Zen and the Art of Mediation' by Martin Plowman |
| 'A Practical Guide to the SRA Principles, Individual and Law Firm Codes of Conduct 2019 – What Every Law Firm Needs to Know' by Paul Bennett |
| 'A Practical Guide to Adoption for Family Lawyers' by Graham Pegg |
| 'A Practical Guide to Industrial Disease Claims' by Andrew Mckie & Ian Skeate |
| 'A Practical Guide to Redundancy' by Philip Hyland |
| 'A Practical Guide to Vicarious Liability' by Mariel Irvine |
| 'A Practical Guide to Applications for Landlord's Consent and Variation of Leases' by Mark Shelton |
| 'A Practical Guide to Relief from Sanctions Post-Mitchell and Denton' by Peter Causton |
| 'A Practical Guide to Equity Release for Advisors' by Paul Sams |
| 'A Practical Guide to Financial Services Claims' by Chris Hegarty |
| 'The Law of Houses in Multiple Occupation: A Practical Guide to HMO Proceedings' by Julian Hunt |
| 'Occupiers, Highways and Defective Premises Claims: A Practical Guide Post-Jackson – 2nd Edition' by Andrew Mckie |

www.ingramcontent.com/pod-product-compliance
Ingram Content Group UK Ltd.
Pitfield, Milton Keynes, MK11 3LW, UK
UKHW020151290926
15471UKWH00004B/800

9 781914 608353